VER POETS'
VOICES

CW01080244

thirtieth anniversary anthology

Edited by May Badman and Margaret Tims

May Badman

*For Harry
with best wishes
15/3/94*

BRENTHAM PRESS

First published 1996 by
Brentham Press 40 Oswald Road, St Albans, Herts ALI 3AQ

ISBN 0 905772 48 2

British Library Cataloguing-in-Publication Data
A catalogue record for this book is available from the British Library

DTP by Gillian Durrant
Printed in England by Watkiss Studios Ltd, Biggleswade, Beds SGI8 9ST

Mary Adcock

SURVIVAL

I think I could survive
If days had no mornings
Heavy with lamentation
Fretted with anger and impatience,
Beginning again the reluctant effort.

I think I could survive
If I could start with afternoons.
Then, the day's length of lethargy
Is past, its noon point of high sun
Penetrating the gloom, giving
Some beams of radiance to the afternoon.

I think I could survive
If I could carry afternoon glow
Like a torch within
So that the small light could grow
To blaze and burn my stupor and reluctance
Lightening the toil, easing my temper,
Warming the heart against cold misunderstanding
And loss of rapport that comes with illness and grief.

Yes, I could survive
If I could hold on to the light
In the mornings.
I could survive.

Previously published in *The Friend*.

Elizabeth Argo

TROGLODYTE

Monday mornings meant
The sheets were changed, the mattress turned,
So every bedroom held a cave
Behind a waterfall
Of bedclothes flung across a chair.
Hiding and the rush from room to room
Was heady fun,
A brief dwindling game
Snatched from the adults
Bent on "getting on".

But late on winter afternoons,
The Sunday lunch long-cleared,
The stove closed down
And adults gone to have their ritual snooze,
The fern-green of the tablecloth
Fringed the caverns of that Xanadu.
Unfathomable depths of dark –
Sanctuary marked by the faint glow
Of anthracite barely sensed
Through the chenille, a dusty warmth,
While high up in the vault
Drips from the black marble cloth
Formed the stalactites of time.

GOD ONLY KNOWS

It was
Only an old thing,
Only an ancient battered object,
Only an item in a list for probate,
Only an unvalued part-lot,
Only an orange lacquered tea caddy,
Only thing that he took with him
When they took him to the hospice.
Only God knows what its worth was.

Pat Arrowsmith

DAVID AND GOLIATH

Moth frail hang-gliders
Breeze buoyed up in hot air hovering;
Or lightly motorized,
Like buzzing insects,
Clockwork toys,
Piloted the simple way.

I am conservative –
Hate and fear sound barrier breaking aircraft,
The rush and roar of Channel Tunnel trains,
Bewildering electronic networks,
Computer driven artificial worlds.

But I would praise and decorate
Those cheeky, metal puncturing woodpeckers
Who sabotaged a hypercomplex rocket
Aiming to probe, explore the universe.

For while we endlessly design
Ever more intricate artifacts and engines
We revere, appear to hanker after nature
And the primitive devices once employed
Decades, centuries ago.

Recently the launch of a space-probing rocket was delayed because woodpeckers
punctured its metal casing.

Pat Arrowsmith

FRIENDSHIP

Friendship –
an entity
of great fragility:
two glass bubbles;
a puff
and they touch;
but the least gust
and they clash,
burst,
are shattered
to infinity.

K. V. Bailey

RIVERS OF LIGHT

The sun we wakened to today
Will spill till dusk its photon flow.
Entropy's debt all stars must pay:
The sun we wakened to today
Is not exempt time will not stay,
Nor will it backwards go – and so
The sun we wakened to today
Will spill till dusk its photon flow.

ONE-WAY TRAFFIC

New Physics says by whirling fast
A time machine can reach the past.
Like a teetotum then I spun,
But found the past was little fun:
A Hole or Death – and both are Black.
How do I get the future back?

FOREWORD

This book is a fitting celebration of the 30th Anniversary of Ver Poets and the poetry it has nurtured and cherished. Elsewhere in this book May Badman outlines the history of Ver Poets. This preface is therefore, and rightly, a celebration of May Badman. For without May Badman there would have been no Ver Poets. She is the founder, creator and the constant sustainer of the group.

It is May, with the support and help of her husband Ray, who has maintained over the years the regular fortnightly meetings, the flow of booklets and news letters, the series of competitions (including the Annual Open Competition with its distinguished winners who include Freda Downie, Carole Satyamurti and Gladys Mary Coles) and the numerous additional readings and bookfairs.

The venues for the meetings have varied from pubs to a rickety old house in Bricket Road, and the now safe haven (thanks to John Mole) of St Albans School. But the attendance and loyalty of members have been constant. It is the friendly and supportive atmosphere, together with a mutual concern for the art and the positive critical approach, all fostered by May, that account for this loyalty and the Ver Poets' successful survival.

May has long been concerned with the art of poetry. I first met her when she was treasurer of the Poetry Society in the sixties. Her work for the art has been recognised by the award of the Howard Sergeant Memorial Prize for Services to Poetry, the Dorothy Tutin Prize for Services to Poetry and her invitation to a Royal Garden Party. In addition May is a fine and sensitive poet in her own right under the name of May Ivimy. Her most recent collection is *Strawberries in the Salad* published by Brentham Press. If you don't know it then you ought to!

A remarkable lady for both her energy and devotion, it has been a privilege to have known May, to have been a member of Ver Poets and to have helped in some small way.

John Cotton
(*President, Ver Poets*)

INTRODUCTION

VER POETS began life in 1966. It was then known as the St Albans & District Poetry Club and came about at the suggestion of St Albans Arts Council when they approached the Verulam Writers' Circle. At that time the Writers' Circle was chaired by Joan Rice; I was their secretary and also a member of the Arts Council.

Joan and I decided to call a public meeting to found the poetry club. As I was a member of the executive council of the London-based Poetry Society we were able to invite the society's programme organiser, Joan Murray Simpson, to come and speak. She was an attractive and eloquent speaker and we finished with the names of thirty interested people.

We formed a small committee and received a grant from St Albans Arts Council of £3 (not quite a useless amount in those days!). We were an active group, all writing, and poetry was at an exciting stage then, very heady times. Finding a permanent home for the club proved to be a serious problem. We were offered a photographic studio, meeting amongst tripods, cameras and back-screens; we tried various public houses, but did not drink enough to please our hosts; then a room in a community centre, sandwiched between a dancing class and a hands-on first aid demonstration. Our numbers fell drastically and it seemed hopeless to try and go on.

However, I thought we could make a fresh start. After some discussion with Ray, my husband, by that time chairman (we were a committee of two – poets generally I found were not very practical and Joan Rice had withdrawn to concentrate on her duties with Verulam Writers' Circle) I decided on a new name, the Ver Poets, and offered membership to people outside the district. Thus we developed with a local and postal membership which covers all of the UK and with members living abroad.

At the same time, we were offered a room in an old house used by the International Centre. This was absolutely central, just behind St Albans City Hall in Bricket Road, and car parking was simple. But no chairs or tables were available. The centre itself, doing splendid work for incoming people from many different nations, was nevertheless operating on a shoe-string. We used the local press to appeal for old furniture which might be lying unused and forgotten in attics and sheds, and during the next couple of weeks gathered in an assortment of chairs and couches, coffee tables, even a carpet of sorts, and soon fitted up our room with a kettle and mugs. We met there for the next ten years.

Then it seemed a pity to use our room only on alternate Monday evenings, and we ran a Poetry Parlour every Saturday from 9 to 4 where poets could call in at any time to read their poems, talk and have coffee. Jeff Cloves (of 'Snorbens Diary' fame in the *St Albans Review*) was a regular visitor, with his guitar, and several other members sang or played. We formed a performing group of poets and musicians with John Mole, Roger Burford-Mason and others, travelling as far afield as Nottingham, Berkhamsted and the Poetry Society in London.

Another project was a stall in St Albans market every Saturday, to sell the poetry pamphlets we were by that time producing, duplicating pages with a jelly-roller and decorating card covers by hand. Concrete poetry was the rage and we had a lot of fun with that, both aurally and 'in print'. The stall was not popular with other stall-holders at first. We did not follow the market conventions and often some of our more youthful members would gather beneath the stall, writing poems and practising their guitars. However, we did eventually make friends, and when rain filled the top of our canvas awning they rallied round to help. We did sell some poetry, and sometimes covered the cost of the stall; but after about three months, with winter coming on, we abandoned that project.

Further changes were to come. The house we were using was condemned on account of dry rot and closed. Fortunately, our member John Mole, by then Vice-President, was teaching English at St Albans School and arranged for us to rent the English Room there. This was full of the right literary atmosphere, lined with books of poetry and I was delighted. Some of the members missed the freedom of Bricket Road, but it was more practical, secure and quiet at the school and we could really write and study there. We have recently moved into the larger English Studio, a lovely light room, which thanks to John Mole and the school we continue to enjoy.

John Cotton has been President of Ver Poets since the early days, and John Mole Vice-President. Other vice-presidents have included Howard Sergeant, editor of *Outposts* magazine, and Roger Burford-Mason who organised our travelling team of poets and musicians, now living in Canada. We are greatly indebted to all who have so acted for their tremendous and ongoing support. And finally, it must not go without saying that my husband and our chairman over so many troubled and untroubled years, Ray Badman, has been a brick throughout.

We now have many established poets as members, as well as beginning writers and those who want to recover the good habits of their youth before the world took over! I feel that poetry is a major part of

British, and Western, culture, involving thought and language and the bringing to bear of objective skill on to the deepest of our emotions. I am very wary of the tendency towards the abuse of sex and violence in the arts, and the loss of respect and esteem generally. But there are great writers today whose work will last, because they are sincere and have not bent the knee to fashion.

Ver Poets' present activities include regular programmes with visiting poets, workshops and competitions. The annual Open Competition is well supported, we produce our pamphlets with a word-processor, and I think I may say we all enjoy our meetings at St Albans School. Postal members are very active, and it is a privilege to help where I can with their work.

May Badman

Publisher's note

When May Badman asked me if Brentham Press would be willing to publish an anthology of members' work to mark the thirtieth anniversary of Ver Poets, I was more than happy to co-operate. Since moving to St Albans from London in 1987 I have been impressed by the consistently high quality of the group's work and by the generosity of spirit that informs all its activities. There seemed to be no more fitting tribute than to provide a platform for the voices of so many talented members to speak to a wider audience. They were not slow to respond to our invitation, resulting in a representative selection from the work of some eighty poets.

The anthology has grown beyond our first expectations into a substantial and, we believe, enduring collection. Ver Poets and Brentham Press are indebted to Eastern Arts Board for financial assistance towards the production of the book, for which our grateful thanks are expressed.

Margaret Tims

CONTENTS

Marjorie Baker

SUN AT MIDNIGHT

At sea where fjords of Norway's Lapland flow
In summer season, where no night can fall
On mountain faces laced in rock-hard snow
Sense anchors on the earth's revolving ball.

The sky is streaked with pearl, and through this cloud
The sun remains in place, controlling all
Its satellites: we spin, our axis bowed.
In summer land and sea, nearest that pole

Always receive its light. There is no dawning
But imperceptible the westering sun
Is veering through the north to east and morning
Sees daylight still: another day's begun.

Here made clear, astronomy shows true
That steady sun that Galileo knew.

THE WORD OF A LAPP

Their language grew in isolation:
Complex, inflected, recognising
Plurality and singularity of twoness,
Insisting on existence of difference;
They make no short cuts with adjectives;
They know that smallness in a reindeer
Is not the same smallness as that of a stone;
Their pebble is nothing like that mighty word –
The rock from which the world was struck:
Lapps are no chatterboxes; their tongue
Is limited to immediate need,
Each word an achievement, heraldic,
Ineffable, the essence of a name.

Patricia Ball

APOLOGY TO E.E. CUMMINGS

i stood at the pearly gates
st. peter smiled at me
"enter" he said

is there bacon and eggs in there?

    no, he said
    oh, i said

is there good red wine, i begged

    no, he said
    oh, i said

dutch butter? wholemeal bread?

    no, he said
    oh, i said

are there sunsets golden red?

    no, he said
    oh, i said

may i stop being dead
and re-incarnate inshtead?

    no such luck, he said

A KIND OF LOVING

Impersonal – no not quite
Loving the essence – yes – not quite.
What do I mean essence?
I cannot say but
not only the essence
the wholeness the presence
hands mouth smile
hunched shoulders slouched stance.

These are the petals I love
enclosing the essence.
What this is I cannot say.

Previously published in *Chatting Now and Then*.

Margaret Banthorpe

SWIMMING LESSON

A huge disused pit where
dark-glass water blank
as a sightless eye
concealed unsounded fathoms —

no shelving beach, no easing
into immersion step by step
only slippery banks of clay
littered with thorny scrub.

My father crouched on a
tiny jut of land. I lowered
into cold untouched
by any ray of warmth.

His hand under my chin
was not enough. I floundered
in his fear, knew that if I sank
I'd plummet too far to surface
for a second chance.

2nd prize, Ver Poets competition 'Aspects of Water'.

Roy Batt

TAKE CARE OF THE POET –
the words will take care of themselves

I do not think I am capable of that sustained order of words
Constituting poetry.
I was told once by a circus manager, that in his experience
Elephants never tap-dance.
 I thanked him for his advice
And wandered off from his caravan
Making my way over guy-ropes
And round cylinders of calor gas.
It was an unknown neck of the woods
The stars were out
And it was dusk

I have come on a lot since then
And after an anthology featuring elephants
In various fulfilling roles
I arrived at a kind of expression a critic called
"Limpid yet firm"

What am I trying to say?
What is it that's really troubling me?
That I want it both ways –
The skills without the discipline,
Fruit without labour,
A stroll around the Pleiades whilst
Playing in the gutter?
And that you would guard my eyes?
Please,
Cover my eyes
Lest the blazing light
Become my night

Mary Blake

THE FLOWER GATHERER

Flute music on the breeze,
violet light of evening
shows her white moth hands
gathering in the darkness
blooms of jasmine
to place beside the bed.

Waking to the sound of rain
she feels cocooned in an underworld
of green, where currents gently
roll her as she trawls
in watery gardens of jellyfish,
passion flowers of the seas,
through drowned starlight
through milky waters,
seeing far above her, half a moon,
she reaches for the jasmine.

INVOCATION

Through the mist of morning
hawthorn trees dance on the edge of the wood
hardly a leaf shows
so weighed down are they in blossom
like mummers in their wicker cages
bringing in the spring with pipes and drum.
Answering the shambling trees
one bird calls, until
the air is smothered in song
louder than a thousand ring of bells
the ancient paean
a canticle to dawn.

Rachel Blake

DOMESTICATED

I ate a pure junket and lived in the nursery –
Till my hot, irksome body precipitated me

Into the kitchen. The burning Aga, the glossed
Wall cupboards insuperably pressed.

At first I was accident-prone. Let slip a jar
– Strawberry jam splashed everywhere,

The sharp shards wounded – it took years to mend.
More settled now, I'm never happier than when

The pots are humming on the stove. Getting
Into the sparkle of a fragile meringue,

A light life with puff pastry. Creating,
I ingest – faint drums of sensation beating.

The meat comes in clear film from the butchery
But the ends of my fingers will touch blood inevitably –

There are knives in the drawers – raw giblets on the table
Yet there's nothing cooking won't render assimilable.

The Aga air induces filmic views
Even so, cooks may hide in chocolate gâteaux –

I have made these walls familiar as skin,
Filtering what goes out, what comes in.

Rachel Blake

FAMILIAR FACES

The honeysuckle horns probe sweetly: I am not ready for death.

Mercury ran through Monica, brightening our consciousness,
Flowing into fiction. All that was withdrawn.
She lived in a timeless world while the days took breath
Endlessly, sitting in a chair, her brain
Lost in a wood. She liked the sun on her back.

Janet saw through the vertigo to the stack
Of the cards against her, the thrombus that waited.
She drove deliberately to Kew with Anne for lunch
And stilled into a statue, still beautiful.

Sylvia sensed strange presences, having to block
Out the world as it is. She opted for sinking.
A virus went along with her logic, invaded,
And metamorphosed her. Death was the terrible crunch.

Yes, they were all warm once. They drop slow.
The dead do not grate on us – their innocence is central.

Tomorrow I go to the wedding, taking from a drawer
Some white gloves I wore once at a funeral.

Previously published in *New Poetry 8* and *Life drawings.*

Grace Blindell

TEMPORARY ARRANGEMENTS

I kneel and plant the fallen conker,
Still as death it lies,
A stillness of unbeing
In the coagulated winter soil.

Yet within that blackened shell,
That dense and hardened flesh,
Flickers an unease – a whisper of memory
Stirs within its clenched and clodded self.

It is the dance, it is the rhythm,
It is the magic alchemy
Which stirs and calls forth struggle,
The conker obeying its habitual path –
Down and up; root and shoot;
A chestnut tree is born.

And yet...
The chestnut tree and I are both
Temporary arrangements.

Morphic resonance whispers memory of being
Whispers pattern but never permanence.
Patterns arise, blend and fade,
The dance shifts and changes,
Intention co-exists with impermanence.

The chestnut tree and I
Are both temporary arrangements.

Yet every seven years or so
I am remade with different stuff,
And what was me...
Becomes (perhaps) the chestnut tree.

Temporarily.

R.A. Bosworth

HERE BE MONSTERS!

Whisper, whisper, mutter, mutter,
From the roof-top to the gutter,
In the door-way, out the shutter –
Rumour flies around.

Is there any truth behind it?
Can we ever hope to find it?
Or pretend that we don't mind it?
Hush now, not a sound.

Do you hear a furtive creeping?
Glimpse a lidless eyeball peeping?
Mortal, turn again to sleeping –
Flee the haunted ground!

Daybreak banishes the dreary
Shadows, dissipates our eerie
Fancies, rumour too grows weary –
Slips away unfound.

Geoffrey Bould

EARTHLY AND DIVINE LOVE

If it's true that logic rules uncurbed
then tell me how to square love's circle
that logic's rule has never curbed
for love pent up in airless prison-cell
escapes, though key-cold logic bars the door,
and finds a mystic path to human hearts
while logic takes insensate thought as king
and marches step by step to self-deceiving answer.
But man's equation is no elegant solution
for still, disdaining logic, mystery remains
to tell us that the human sum
is greater than its parts, and logic dull
needs God's love divine to work through mine
and make the earth divine, though earthly.

Previously published in *Quaker Monthly* and *Beehive Press Anthology*.

John Bourne

LANDFALL, GRENADA
(for Louis Cox – garden boy)

Now in your perennial bed,
Where the spicy fume of nutmeg
Foams over the silver shore,
Tantalizing mariners with the
Culmination of their quest.

A feather of cirrus floats over
Grand Etang, lost in the
Deep pool of mountain forest;
Your garden, on the rocky bluff
Above the sea, prolific in
Daily globes of tomatoes,
Cassava, Ochra;
Your prehensile toe pulled you
Up the vertical slopes, where
You slashed tarantula weeds,
While carrying the cloud of a
Watering can, to rain on
Parched terraces.

Who knows where is your rotting dust,
The topsoil of a volcanic island,
Who drinks the fiery juice to your memory,
In the bar on the careenage,
From where the schooners sailed,
Beyond the horizon of your imagination,
Under the bluff of your domain.

Suzanne Burrows

ROMAN CHILD

On the last turn of the stair,
under the skylight, looking up.
Clouds racing from the moon
pull from consciousness
sudden simultaneous thoughts:

Parmenides' precept: *Being Is,*
and the sight of the roman child's
bleached skeleton – colour of moonlight –
the fragile bones sprawled in the grave,
ribs fallen fan-like; a mandala
where the heart had rested.

Buried with treasure:
a necklace of blue glass beads,
one samian urn, one durovingian bowl.

Little enough to us, her secret.
The small imperishables close to bone,
the bone, near to moonlight,
the flesh, grass growing towards light.

Previously published in *Vision On.*

Maggie Cain

GARDEN

There is respite here at evening
from the fevered rush of living

> lavender and jasmine, rose de mai

from the burden of achieving
the drudgery of earning

> foxglove, lady's mantle, columbine

from power games, the scheming
the role and status seeking

> roses falling over sun-warmed stone.

I return here in the evening
from immeasurable distance

> paths of camomile and creeping thyme

trailing honeysuckle

harebell

heartsease.

Marjorie Carter

MAKING ROOM

All that happened was he took her hand
on Aldeburgh beach when her feet stumbled,
numb from the sea – only that: astounding her
with remembered sureness.

And the sealed door cracked,
the sigh uncoiled from its long ache,
light broke in ribbons against her face
beckoning her back from dream.

Since then she's been moving the furniture,
turning out cupboards, changing the pictures,
throwing things away,
making room.

Previously published in *Vision On.*

Margaret Caunt

ART MASTER

Always a teacher has a head start;
he knows his subject and you don't.
I was astonished over the years
to see uncertainty lurking beneath the mask;
gifts such as his should surely breed
assurance. The pipe and mug of coffee
gave passing comfort, but when mislaid
work ceased till they were found.

Able but unassuming, forthright and kind
he supported my indifferent talent,
tendrils holding to an established tree
whose roots were down, secure.
His nature's symphony had edge
but even the clashing notes lent colour.
Always the architecture of his mind
leaned to dynamic form, forced pictures
to speak – technique was not enough.

Scathing of trivial themes,
"kittens in baskets", yet
his strength held at the heart
a tenderness and high
regard for artists down
the ages who knew the way
to capture fire.

Previously published in *No Sense of Grandeur*.

A.C. Clarke

SPIRIT ANCESTOR

I sang across the sands of Australia
The song flew out of my mouth
Ahead of me, spread wings over
Dry track, hatched boulder and thorntree.
I sang my land into shape.

A sliver of sharpened bone
A bagful of magic

I danced along the sands of Australia
Wove my steps into north and south
Saw the watersnakes wriggle and quiver
The sandhill rise into high rock under me
I danced my land into shape.

Caves of the ancestors
Recumbent forms
Rainfurrowed cheeks

I dreamed above the sands of Australia
Set my thumb upon rainland and drouth
Seeded myself in my sisters for ever
Coiling from sea to sea
I dreamed my land into shape.

Cockatoo plumes on a songless skull
Dancing feathers
Dreams in the lightless caverns
My ancestral smile.

A.C. Clarke

FACING IT

If winter comes, we say
willing expected spring,
new-sapped growth
from deadwood desires,
resurrection of buried resolve.

Every cloud we say
watching the hammerheads
bruise eggshell blue
and a finger of light
strike downwards, suggesting salvation.

The king is dead, we say
waiting to welcome the heir.

Life goes on we say
each time the door clangs shut
behind another exit.

It is coming all the same
the tongue-tied time
breath shaken loose from its folds
throat's last spasm
gagging on failed air.

Let me word it now,
heave into solid sound
the slab beyond the strength of angels,

squat monosyllable
at the mouth of silence.

Gladys Mary Coles

KATHERINE MANSFIELD'S MIRROR (CHALET DES SAPINS)

A chalet of the old type, cuckoo-clock roof,
ornate, the balcony creaking;
and the view she saw each day
across to the Weisshorn above Sierre —
these I saw too, as with her eyes.
The perpetual snows, the vines in neat plots:
it's hardly changed at all since she was there,
since her bid to cure her lungs in Alpine air.
'*Oui, c'est le même*,' the concierge nods,
key-laden, at the door, '*aussi les sapins*'.
Evergreens, omnipresent, guard the chalet —
'the last romantic thing left in Montana'
wryly the concierge smiles, takes me up
to Katherine's room, her balcony, her mirror.
The mirror in its wooden frame
on a wall between two windows:
I move forward eagerly, look — and look away,
and cannot stand in front, not wanting to imprint
my own reflection on this glass. It should be kept
unlooked in, any vestige of her glance preserved
like the high snows, unvisited and pure.
And then a deeper reason shows its face:
I am afraid: in this mirror at her disease
she stared, seeking the trace of a Colonial girl
in the troughs of her dark eyes. My own lungs
weak, prey to the wheeze of allergy, I fear
her stark reality in that mirror: in there
I might fall and sink, be swallowed
in her consuming truth.

1st prize: Ver Poets, Michael Johnson Memorial Poetry Competition.

Gladys Mary Coles

LEAFBURNERS

move quietly as smoke
to their mounds; brush
rhythmically, apply spikes
to the invoices of winter,
papery tokens of decay

others wield spades like spoons
with the ease of breakfasters
shovelling cornflakes

when the pyre is high
they strike matches avidly:
in the wind of flames
dry leaves curl, given movement
for the last time

usually at dusk, gathering
in the corners of gardens,
servants to impalpable fire
they feed the autumn bier

eyes blazing with immolation,
their office skills, creeds, degrees
fall away, severed boughs
tossed to crackle, burn
and, in burning, change

the earth the air receives

Previously published in *Leafburners*.

John Cotton

QUARTIER BENAUD
(La Chaise Dieu)

Out there the one street lamp rinses
The cow-pat patinaed road and rough stone walls
With a light in which the shadows come off best.
All is quiet except for the pulses of trees,
The house's small complaints,
The breathing of a darkness pricked with stars.
Dogs are having uneasy dreams of their peers,
One punctuates the night with a metronome of barks.
Awakened we fend off memories of failure
As they ease their way to envelop us.
Morning will bring the chatter
                                of hunch-shouldered martins
Preening before they carve the sky's feast.
Flies are already whingeing in the kitchen.
Then the soft-shoe shuffle of the gentle eyed cows
Who grant as they pass their epiphany
Of a sweet sickly incense of fructifying dung,
While the mellow abbey bells toll of redemption.

Previously published in *Ambit*.

John Cotton

ARMISTICE DAY

Was it all those elevens that did it?
The eleventh month, the eleventh day,
Even the hour, and my Father's life
Punctuated by stays in hospital
As the metal worked out of his wounds,
Then the "daft" (he was buried alive) uncle.
It all added to that peculiar mystery
As we stood behind our desks at school,
Flanders poppies bright in our lapels,
Knowing that the world had fallen quiet,
The police had held up the traffic,
People stood still in the street,
Shops stopped serving, the postman on his round
Poised statued while we all listened
In the suburbs to the distant guns
Firing their salutes in Hyde Park.
Armistice Day, *Never, never again*
Was the message echoing across the shires.
If only we could learn as easily.

John Cotton

THE ALL-NIGHT DINER
(For Edward Hopper)

A small oasis of light in the darkened street,
The diner has its own histories,
The mini-dramas of a theatre
With a shifting cast and one set.
Its presence is what matters:
Its offer to share a distilled loneliness.
Old Luigi has worked there for thirty-eight years,
Seventeen of those tortured by a mis-treated hernia,
Better the pain you know,
The sadness of empty tables,
Discarded hopes that gather like dust,
The old familiar air patinaed
With ancient garlics and steamings.
He is thankful for the warmth
And the reassurance of self.
There are the memories:
The old regular
Who would fall asleep over his soup,
The later comers
Escaping from the cold indifference of streets,
And the occasional new customer,
Sometimes a small brief comet of brightness
Leaving a lingering scent
That stirred dreams that never were.
We'd miss the light from this place,
Glimpsed at through its plate glass.
Sometime we will moth towards its refuge.

John Coutts

IN PRAISE OF THE GIRLS' BATH-HOUSE AT
AKAI SECONDARY SCHOOL, NIGERIA
(and in memory of Evangeline Cooper)

Listen! Half a
Lifetime after:
Chuckling water –
Splashing laughter!

First the modest
Green enclosure
(Only fronds
Denied exposure)

Then a concrete
Soaping palace
Freed our girls
From lust or malice.

Liverpool ladies
Prayed together:
Sponsored zinc
To fool the weather.

Maids with pails
Paraded grinning.
Righteousness for once
Was winning.

Other shrines
Receive ex-votos:
We got by
With Kodak photos.

Grandma filed
Our snaps with care.
Now her flat
Is blank and bare.

"Helping Hands!"
The caption states:
She who reigns
With all-time greats –

Springs a truth
Beyond all seeming:
Laughing Ruth
With bucket gleaming.

Sponsored poem for Christian Aid Week, May 1995

Penny Cutler

STORM CLOUDS

The wind has been blowing storm
clouds nearer for days.
Birds linger less in the garden
preferring tall chimneys
to low borders.

Fish flick tails,
weave through tangled weed
as pond reflections wrinkle into
distorted faces.

It is almost here.
Giant proportions
begin to overshadow.

There must be no more delay or debate.
It will not slow down or go away.
There is no other course of action.
This storm will wait no longer.
It is here.

Alan Dunnett

IN BED WITH MACBETH

I hear him now, the candle gutters
On his wrist. I can't close my eyes,
The bone-rings clench my jaw, it stutters
Inside the skull, cold water in drips.

He puts his back to me and sighs
Like a mouse lamed in a trap –
Every night the same but neither cries,
Staring and apart in one big coffin.

I take my hand and make it slip
Between his legs, to stop the thinking.
He twists his neck and bites my lips,
Our gooseflesh chafes the bed-fur.

He drags my head down to his lap
And knots my hair in his fist.
A child calls twice and the moon wraps
Herself in a mist for shame.

If I held a cup now, I'd let it sip
Until I were drowned in the drinking.
I'd take my hands and make them dip
In the wine to make the nails clean.

If I held a knife now, I'd let it drive
Between my eye and my crack.
If I were a child and called out twice,
Would my mother come for my sin?

I hear him now, he groans and mutters,
And swears by his Christ as he lies.
And now he starts his dead man's shudders,
Whilst I brood my sores to the quick.

Previously published in *The Methuen Book of Theatre Verse*.

Alan Dunnett

PROSPERO IS SAD WITHOUT ARIEL

I was waiting for you, Ariel, not at the usual place,
Of course, and with no book to unlock
And chant at, as Caliban would have it.

I was looking at the evening clouds, Ariel,
And wondering if you were running along their ridges,
Across the red light and smoke and shadows.

Ariel, I thought you were in the room just now,
Behind me, laughing like an echo of icicles
Chimed by the wind, but when I turned, you were gone.

Do you think of me at any time, Ariel –
Perhaps when your wings creak and I am not there
To oil them, and unruffle your feathers?

I want to talk to you, Ariel, your peculiar listening
Made me bright, as if you were an attentive unicorn,
And I were Merlin on holiday.

Ariel, your perfume was wet pine and earth, sometimes,
Or traces of musk. I brushed your shoulder in passing,
And kissed the air, as you flew on your way to be free.

Previously published in *Orbis*.

Judith Everitt

AUBADE

Distant transistors hoot and chuckle,
A milk van hums, and clinks a bottle –
The sound, though not the sense, of words:

Blackbirds on gables flute and bustle,
And kittens mew and scratch and scrabble,
And catch at pips and curtain-cords,

And cheerful hinges squeak in cupboards,
And mantel clocks tick tittle-tattle –
The sound, though not the sense, of words;

And spotted starlings trip and jostle,
And strop their beaks, and click, and hustle –
Swoop down and case the grass in hoards,

Gas pops and hisses under kettles,
A young child wakes, and cheeps, and prattles –
His voice hops lighter than a bird's –

The sound, though not the sense of words.

Gillian Fisher

DUELS OF WIND INSTRUMENTS

Both clarinet and flute, likewise
Took plain air, as each player breathed –
And by some alchemy, did splice
That air with melody, though sheathed
In two long steins of steel and wood,
From where our ears drank, while they could.

Who had the lioness's share
Of Ponchielli's *Dance of Hours?*
Neither one of them would dare
Profess she had. Harsh judgement sours
Or would, the duo's amity,
What a musical calamity!

A splendid hour lingered, and
Sped on its way, at Music's rates
Progressing better than they'd planned,
Despite white-knuckle nervous states
About the risk of faulty notes.
Their tunes would honour blackbirds' throats.

Dorothy Francis

BLACKBERRY PICKING

Occasionally,
When I find myself alone
Away from the other blackberry pickers
I become afraid and suddenly turn round
In the quiet field
By the quiet hedge
In the broad day's light.

And I turn to face
Infinity
Or slanted eyes smiling
Gold dusted, beguiling,
Or— long furry ears.

And suddenly, self conscious
I shout, "Wait for me."
As I hurry away from
Eternity,
From the precipice,
From the hummocks of green
And the spinning Down.

To a welcoming arm that
Waves to me, calls
"Here we are."
Ah this is the way that is known to me
And I gladly return.

I gaze at the other blackberry pickers:
I smell the wine of the blackberry:
I frown upon fears of sharp, furry ears,
And ban immortality.

Joan Fry

THOMAS AQUINAS
"Dumb ox, his lowing would be heard all over the world...."
                              Albertus Magnus c. 1200-1280

Expensively educated at Monte Cassino
And the new University of Naples
He came of knightly Aquinine stock

A smart ox lowing in a superior byre.

But then was caught up with those black Dominicans,
Mendicant, malodorous.
Pursued parentally, was captured, imprisoned.

Ox ignominiously tethered on the Rocca Secca.

His writing grew cramped, obscurely abbreviated.
Friars, being poor, economise on parchment.
Returned to studies and austerities, he grew perversely fat:

A rolypoly ox on a black-coped outcrop.

"Summa contra Gentes" laid aside
He went out, amongst nearer gentes in Anagni, Rome,
Viterbo, Orvieto and other orotundities.

Old Aristotelian ox grazing in a new Christian orchard.

"The Summa Theologica" fell in five thick volumes.
Reason and Faith embraced platonically in its pages.
Prim imprimatur sanctioned universities' cataloguing.

The ox ruminated five proofs of God's existence, a comprehensive cud.

In France His Corpulence fell suddenly silent
Then thumped with thick fist on the royal table:
"That's finished the heresies of the Manichees!"

The ox rudely lowing oblivious of rich pasturage.

On December the sixth a divine revelation.
What came before, he said, was like so much straw.
He wrote nothing about it, nor after it.

The ox, snuffing the vision, scuffed the dry despised stalks.

Dumb ox, whose lowing vibrated through medieval stalls
Scuttling the pin-head schoolmen.

Muriel Gibson

DISTANT RELATIONS

They are too quiet in the garden now:
no lively conversation, sharp dissent;
the words have all been said.

He's sluggish in his movement,
bends his back, stiff-legged,
to water the geraniums;
she, inert, follows the spider's silver thread,
knitting discarded; then offers tea,
cups it in crooked hands,
slops it impatiently across the table.

Cap over eyes he slouches in his chair, snoring;
silent, she ruminates on trivialities.

Previously published in *Envoi.*

Ray Givans

LETTER HOME
(An imagined account in which Sylvia Plath resides in Belfast)

Dear Mother,

We have purchased the most heavenly house imaginable;
I wish you could visit us at once!
And the people we've met in Ireland are so amiable,
I can feel my whole being quite flourish.

I just knew this was home, like a person with whom I converse;
Already it responds to my touch,
the green linoleum gone, ochre more sensitive to the light;
fastidious, yes, but lifts the spirits.
Ted at once ear-marked one bedroom as a temporary study,
painted the walls a fresh apple green,
finished the natural table and furnished with sturdy chairs
(local auction $80)

The gardens are a blessing; lined with productive apple trees,
vegetable plot – self-sufficient,
and flowers: petunias, zinias, laburnum, honeysuckle....
Oh for spring's rash of color and scents,
this space and air so fine, little Frieda needs two naps a day.

Mrs McCracken is coming for tea; quite a local figure.
Her husband, (retired) mortuary chief,
put me in touch with a sweet young doctor at the Health Centre;
such a marvellous free health service.

Here, winter's slate gray rain envelops me, and I feel rather low,
and the my soul is restitched, again,
on fine days – the garden is such a tapestry of color.
I take solace in my dear husband,
and my little angel, her smiles dappled with luscious dimples;
my whole life will affirm songs of joy.

Love,
Sivvy

Ray Givans

WHEN TWO LIVES MEET

Opposite, the woman scrubs as she kneels;
And from his wheelchair she seems pathetic
As her ungainly body grinds on wheels
Driven by inbred Protestant ethic.

She fills days with lists of chores completed.
Never sleeps; yet, at night, dreams by the fire;
Only her emotions are depleted,
Surrogate mother, work, feeds her desire.
And in her living is content.

Stooped, at work, she watches a life cheated
And has pity for inert arms and legs.
She thinks how his life must be depleted
For without work, he sits dog-bowed and begs.

And yet his mind wanders through wilderness,
Sure-footed where great men sought enlightenment.
Even in his dreams he is whole no less
Than when he walked upright, with thoughts head bent;
And in his being is content.

Previously published in *Acumen*.

Daphne Gloag

THE VISIT
Children born after their mothers had a kidney transplant
meet the Minister

The camels might never have been here.
They stand tall and indifferent
while the children climb between their humps.
The government minister holds a baby; mothers
are almost blooming and carefree. They possess the day.
Minister, Minister, shout the photographers,
look this way please. Camels dying
in deserts are far and forgotten nearly.

Beyond the zoo wind tangles
in precarious grass, temporary daffodils
are suddenly remarkable. The day of camels,
warm camel breath, and the ugly convenient humps
are irreplaceable. A moon faced mother,
amused, absorbed, holds up her child
to the camel's brown, comfortable hair,
straggling, undeniable.

Previously published in *Poems from the Medical World* and *Diversities of Silence.*

Hilda Groom

IMMORTALITY

In many city parks,
Chiselled statues
wearing sparrow marks,
Confirm
Immortality.

Baby new,
I saw you,
in sweet repose
There – immortality
was mine,
by
    a
        nose.

Elsie Hamilton

TO MY BROTHER

Hours can be made
to punctuate,
but now it is words
beating under the loop of days,
breaking up into
the seventh, then
ducking down again.

It's not so much
what they say
as the voice they
come alive in,
linking me
with the child that I was
and the warm past.

Elsie Hamilton

THE OTHER CHILDREN

This grass is still disturbed
by their running feet;
the air still moved
by their voices.
Joyful, without self-knowledge.

The breeze is full of them
blown about and dancing,
tearing over the climbing-frame
and down the slide;
so many of them peeping
between the children of today.

In this place
they never change
or go away;
their laughter and their tears
are sunshine and bright rain
falling on cherished ground.

Alan Hardy

LIFE

My father's face serious-sets a concrete shocked gloom;
he sits there staring throughingly at his sons' families' conversations,
numb-smacked by his unanticipated sniffing of death
on the operating-table's reneged minor cutting-up.

He never was I must say much a man for words,
never someone who felt he had to achieve,
just a smoker who watched plenty of TV.

But his hands-pocketed pacing up and down, slow-frantic,
and his head-falling baby's sudden stupor on reaching bed-time,
and his frightened-eyed blindness to all around
in his all-senses-touching taste of mortality,
makes him stone-facedly inwardly wince
at the realisation that what he will one day lose
is as precious to him as
that which drove Michelangelo and Shakespeare on.

Previously published in *Envoi*.

Joyce Haynes

TO MARY AND JOHN....

Night time and the roads are ribbed with silence
From its curtained home
A single light beats lonely bars of labour
Stars attend the angled roofs of stone.

Riding high the moon speaks peace to poets
Crushing reason to its dust of bone
Travelling uncharted seas of vision
Gilding wisdom's undiscovered dome.

Night time and the single light is beaming
Life against the darkness of the womb
Press of flesh and thresh of limb is flooding
Red and warm the dryness of the tomb.

Shooting stars break up the mesh of heaven
Split a passing atom
Light a home.

Here a woman waits another spasm
Here a man forgets his need to roam.

Previously published in *Vision On.*

Christopher Highton

VICIA HIRSUTA
('Hairy Tare')

'Flowers insignificant, pale lilac, in a long-stalked spike of 1 to 6,
with long slender calyx-teeth' — *The Pocket Guide to Wild
Flowers* by David McClintock and R.S.R. Fitter.

Take up your lens, hold still,
Move gently in until
Confusion approaches focus,
Suddenly snaps sharp, discloses
A textured moon whose grace
Frames a flower's face
In filaments of light.

Two purple almond eyes
Fringed on each side
With wings of luminous silk
Stare unblinking back.
Five calyx fingers cup
This art, offer it up
As if to beguile.

Gathered closely round,
Matching blooms peer out
Like haloed choirboys frozen
In mid-anthem, open-
Mouthed, eager to raise
Again their song of praise
Before your eyes.

May Ivimy

REPETITIONS AND DEVIATIONS

Each day I feed the cats and birds
And grieve in passing that I have not hoovered the house for ages
And have bought too many books and
Too many plants in pots and too many clothes,
And haven't been to church nor prayed exactly
But I do think, yes, I think and wonder
And ponder about all these wars
And starvations and people in Africa and London
With no money and nowhere to live, and
I think it is not good literature to have all these 'ands'
And no conclusion, and how can there be
When the great question behind it all remains unsolved,
Like has God seeded just this one small globe with intelligent
beings
Is earth the only green oasis in a universe of fire
And dead rock, and is God?
Is He? and if not is it worth while
Struggling to turn our course around
From cruelty, destruction and war?
I am not alone, except that every I is alone,
Millions of us, sparks of existence, each
Caged in our flesh, driftwood in a cataract
And only the falls ahead
Which reminds me
Today, I must wash my hair.
Near as we are to Hell, we are near to Heaven,
And I would be clean.

May Ivimy

POEM FOR THE NEW YEAR

The long, thin, morning shadows
Across the frosty field,
The big brown horse, his dark tail
And the small cream patch on his belly
Lit up and rounded
By the first keen sunlight
Of the New Year. Oh,
How much we are going to do,
Beautifully do, in the name
Of all this precise and formal vigour of beauty,
The cared-for field, the neat-spread ice,
The warm, solid horse,
Noble as he stands
In the sun.

ABSENCE AND RETURN

The room below, when I went down
Sang of my absence. The light seemed wrong,
Old newspapers made a disorder, crockery, clean
But misplaced, yielded a strangeness, and the cat
With hang-dog, soulful eyes, seemed hungry
But would not eat.

Hands eager to make amends, I
Heaved newsprint, gathered letters,
Read the milkman's note, watered
Two drooped-flat plants,
Laid a tray,
And began to feel forgiven.

M.A.B. Jones

MARCH JOURNEY

But for the jumbled hills crowding around,
red soil running south, you could have said
Cuyp making his picture-magic of some
Dutch landscape. There was no haze –
the day light, bright as the heart of summer.
Cattle stood frackled, statuesque
on flat pastures, grazed Welsh Borderland
in stock attitudes of painted ease.

From the train, not a ruin in sight.
The March, once moated, fortified,
lay to the west .... Hard, on that day –
young winter corn drilling peaceable fields,
a plough sailing brown seas in a cloud of dust –
to credit the turbulent past. No sign
of earthwork mound, square keep, the scene
imperturbable, staid. Those age-old
skirmishes buried deep.

And as, unheard through glass, a dizzy lark
fluttered its spiral into the high unseen,
the diesel, speeding past farmyards, trees,
reaped a first harvest
of green after green.

Pauline Keith

RETURNING

Too soon.
The sun of Lesbos burns in me
under the cooling of my skin
to Englishness.

My eyes still watch black bees
disappearing down the bells
of blue convolvulus. My feet
feel the flop of sandals
worn to their breaking point
and left, symbolic, on a wall
by the road to Eressos.

You may think I am back
but I'm not yet at home.

Previously published in *The Inquirer*.

SWALLOW AT WASDALE HEAD

Unlooked for – its flash unseen –
My eye busy with a barn and the swell
Of the ridge-route clambering Kirk Fell:
The farmyard and the hill arranged between
An overhanging, dark-leaved frame
And the rough stone where I stooped,
Intent on composition. I took no aim
At him. He chose when he swooped
For the eaves – a fraction of his line
Caught at one five-hundredth by my lens,
Its gaze encompassing much more than men's
Selective sight: I can't call this photo mine.

Behind me, I remember, you
From the south, a swallow too.

Previously published in *Poet's England: Cumbria*.

Hannah Kelly

DAYLIGHT

Daylight in Honfleur dawns in at five,
Painters at their easels near the boats,
The light is golden in the evening sky,
The cafes and umbrellas drifting by.
Professor and his pupil sit and talk,
Books on Baudelaire, The Odyssey,
While promenaders take the air and walk —
Professor, famous name, and earned.

The light in the Bassin
Is golden now, a painter's Paradise,
With beer and gherkins, onions, Wurst,
The books rotate, the evening light is there.

Honfleur for painters, poets, men
Of letters, daylight calls you then.

Previously published in *Outposts* and *The Silver Snake*.

Robert Knee

HIGH NORFOLK

Becalmed on this great lung
Of far seen stretching air,
Back-dropped by skies deep-
Draughted with autumn hues.
I catch the dark crowded
Spinneys of the night,
Open casts of tree and hedge-
Infusing oxygen, feeding sight.
Inland, gaunt tombstones
Of church tower, scattered,
Bereft, irregular shadows,
Waymarkers to the old,
Sought by few but the passing;
Kestrels, walkers, sails,
Alone in this forgotten sigh
Of mazed, neglected trails.

Gillian Knibbs

TREEFELLING

In the half light, crowds of twigs
Crawled the lawn and branches rolled
As if in their final death throes.
Red berries squashed on the stone patio.
You scurried up from the shed,
Brushing leaves and wiping manly sweat.

Your eye caught mine expecting praise.
I dealt you silent hate. That night,
With curtains left undrawn,
I watched the vacant sky and mourned
My naked tree, for fifteen years
The keeper of moon-filtered thoughts and dreams.

Early next morning, you swung
Awkward from the shivering trunk,
Hung on some breeze-blown rope. I could
Hardly bear to watch but with each thud
Of severed wood, you slipped slowly
To safety, my father, the vanquisher.

Lotte Kramer

THE GURU OF GROCERIES

In my grandfather's town,
In a corner shop,
The smell of spices bounced from the walls,

The goods in a jumble
Of tubs and jars
From fresh Sauerkraut to a mêlée of sweets.

We would skip all the way
To be greeted there
By a soft young man in a kosher-white coat:

The guru of groceries;
He ruled his domain
With his silhouette mother in a velvet back room.

Many children from school
Dropped in on their way
For a bag of sweets, a chat and a smile,

Till one day he had gone;
The shutters were down,
The place was as dead as a drowned house.

Only trickling whispers
Explained with much grief
His forbidden love, his fragile sin

With a girl, not a Jew,
Who had stayed too long.
And we never ever saw him again.

Note: any relationship between Jews and Gentiles was prohibited in Nazi Germany.
Previously published in *Ambit*.

Lotte Kramer

ERNST LUDWIG KIRCHNER IN DAVOS, 1920-1938

Not as an outcast
He came at first
But as a constant convalescent.

He settled at the edge
Of a quiet-green valley
Rounded by a waterfall

Where his feverish knife
Carved spiky woodcuts
Of stones, trees and peasant life.

His carnival brush
Returned a landscape
To fearless adventures.

The harshness subdued.
Women's faces like lanterns
Under black hats,

Their bodies starched
They stand in threes
In a spring meadow.

His colours are new
Lighting skies are pierced
By sharp-ribbed mountains,

The village a refuge,
Bright with dancing houses
And never-ending steeples;

The shooting bodies
Of girls riding in rhythms
To ascending clearness,

Yet his own earth stays hostile.
His exit as outcast:
His last determined statement.

Note: the art of E.L. Kirchner was prohibited as 'degenerate' in Nazi Germany.
He committed suicide in 1938.

Previously published in *Ambit*.

Keith Lewis

CROFT

The day they left,
was it like this – grey
with the threat of rain in the wind?
Stooping under this sullen lintel
sour-faced, cursing,
or silent, picking a sprig
of parsley, listening to the sea
and a peewit keening?
                Perhaps
in the sometime sun
a peach-cheeked baby woke
to the wheep and shriek of a kettle,
and under the once-taut washwire
now swarfed in tousled grasses by
the rusted pump, where his long
johns clowned in the sea breeze
with her bloomers,
a child scolded her dolls,
hearing, maybe, his saw
rasp and burr in the cluttered outhouse
or the tractor churring as it clawed
furrows in the bleak fields above
the bay.
     Only the whine of the wind
as it claps the latch
of a wrecked shutter,
and the distant
muttering of thunder, as
                   far out
on the water's glaucous reaches,
a school of dolphin mark leisurely,
casual circumflexes.

Mari Louth-Cook

RABBITS IN THE MOONLIGHT

you phoned
when you reached home;
told me the solution to
twenty down
that came to you
as you drove
the fifteen miles to Alresford;

repeated the fond murmurings
that were our sustenance
in those lean times
of little contact:
our manna in the desert.

described
the magic of the moon-bathed
world; the luminous summered
trees; the silvered rabbits
courting in the fields,
as you drove up Magdalen Hill.

Susanne Lutz

NARCISSUS

    I am divine
How can I bear the staring crowd
Their vulgar glances detracting from my beauty day by day?
And he skilfully unhinges his head
Takes it off his shoulders
Clasps it with his right arm
And gently presses his face against his chest

One never ends exploring oneself
To feel my nose poke in my ribs
    what a fillip
And he gives his head an affectionate hug

Heads are not good for much
Mine shall be saved from getting used and worn
Thus I will wear it only very rarely
On opportunities I cannot do without

    And he struts away
    A well-built trunk
    On two legs
    An elegant torso
    With a butt of a neck
Like the statues found in excavations

Kevin Maynard

LIBER NATURAE

Driving through the Hautes-Alpes:
winter mud;
summer dust.

Içi la Bibliotheque —
Scrawled on a cardboard placard
Stuck to a battered door,
Half wrenched off its hinges —

Just before the village *cimitière*.

What do they read down there?

The same stone book
That weather writes on
Storm by storm,
Age by age...

The book of starlight and slow time
That crumbles into stillness

And whose stillness never ends.

W.A. Mellors

VIEW FROM CLEVELEYS

The concrete promenade stretches and glowers
At the wind-led hostile sea, sweeping the shelves
Of pebbles, moving with an automatic growl
Louder than the flower destroying wind.

Exact along its line of longitude
Wary, that straight edged coast glares at the west.
At the sometimes glimpsed three legged Isle of Man
As the Irish Sea swallows the setting sun.

Blackpool, south a few bare miles, where the tower
Is based on its promenade of promises,
Difficult to catch. They slip through the fingers
Like old pennies in the slot machines.

Blackpool with its Punch and Judy on the golden sands.
Its Pleasure Beach of noise and whirling wheels.
I hold fast to my warm cloak of nostalgia
To revisit the past on that cold coast.

Look north. The lost industry of Barrow
Stretches to the sea its ghostly fingers.
But beyond, older far than the metal tower
The concrete promenade and deserted shipyards
The bulk of Black Combe, beckoning to where behind
Lie all the hills and lakes of Cumbria.

David Message

ICON

Colour and light
Image and space
Inner and outer
Onlooker and face

Seeking forgiveness
Looking for power
Perceiving goodness
Observing a flower

Knight and shepherd
Heaven and hell
War and peace
Silence and the bell

Eyes to the left
Eyes to the right
Eyes to the centre
Keep you in sight.

Previously published in *The Old Rectory.*

John Mole

HIGH SUMMER

Too hot to sleep even at midnight
with a little breeze now
and the streetlights off
we walk around the block, old-stagers
of romance, my warm hand
on your naked shoulder.

Others are out too
in this turn-about dissolve
to early morning, shadows
of themselves with
assignations burning
but beyond recall.

My hand slips down
to lace our fingers
while so much to come
is haunting here
between my footsteps
and the pattern on your dress.

TONIGHT

Across the table, our hands
meet in romantic fiction,
palm down, their fingers
mounting each other.
Whatever licence we allow
is not what the eye sees.

Say nothing. Let be
the fact of the matter.
Thirty years and still
with luck like this
is a dream to wake to.

John Mole

NEL MEZZO DEL CAMMIN

One old bean to another
At a Literary party: *I saw you*
In the pub before we got here
And said to myself that's an old bean
I recognise but don't recall
His name. Who are you? Yes
Of course. I thought
We were both dead. Delighted.

And you? The two of them
Have turned to me. I tell them
I'm a middling bean, past fifty
But not much. They raise their glasses
Here's to youth, and what do
You write? Poetry, I tell them.
Jolly good they say, *Delighted.*
Do you rhyme? Who are you?

So the party goes, so many glasses
Raised to this and that, to faces
Glimpsed across the room, then
Home. A nightcap as my son
Comes last thing from a pub
Where all the young beans gather
Knowing everyone. *Enjoy yourself?*
We ask each other. *Jolly good!*

Jillian Mounter

VJ DAY

I had attained the ripe old age of three.
My mum was walking down the street with me.
I said:- "I do not like the Japanese".
Mum looked at me aghast and said:- "Jill, please!
Since last weekend the Japs have been our friends."
So learned I young how suddenly war ends.

Previously published in *First Time Magazine*.

Olive R. Nathan

SPRING - 1988

With each spring
Come all springs
I ever can remember;

With surprise
Another April
Follows last September,

And arise
New phoenix
From pale winter's ember.

Previously published in *Symphony*.

Ruth Partington

VIEW FROM THE TELEFERIQUE

The mountains, softly blue,
So still, remind me,
The birds, flying soundlessly
In this airy place,
Remind me –
In spite of the buzz
Of the song machines,
The voices of the radio,
The click of knives and forks,
The memories flooding in my mind,
In spite of the red geraniums,
The red of the café chairs,
The blue and white,
The stillness, the silence,
Remind me –
I am alone.

Brian Louis Pearce

AT THE SUPERMARKET

On the longest day, I
came pushing my trolley
past water- and honey-
dew melon, bleach, canned veg
and pineapple: took my
ticket to joy via the
delicatessen. Three
bells tinkled on the edge

of my billed thoughts. I saw
the lights hung over us
in trios and I watched
with worship three wise doors
open to let the four
apocalypse boys suss
out the rain-front that scotched
Lamb-time at Lords. Applause

round the check-outs. They must
have opened all twelve to
appease the swarming folk
stretched long-lined and queue-tame
back to "fruit", or adjust-
ed the belts to speed you. Pew-
ed by the unstained glass, invoke
higher powers, kneel and claim

vision before leaving:
discount from above, be
it the eclipsed voice-over.
I'm for the road again,
a spent peasant plodding
with bailiff's bags up the
long causeway and over
the bridge, bent against rain.

Brian Louis Pearce

KEW GLASS

Escape from the hard laugh,
conned in the glass city
over the bar glass, to
the white light, green suffused
in the glass of Kew. Scarf-
armed against spit pity
from scud clouds, blush of true
English June the glass mused

on this morning, go in
and dissolve in the green
abundance, the yellow-
sweet petals of broom, smell
and swell of the jasmine,
felt odour of thyme, screen-
scene of grace, the fellow
of Paradise. All's well

if it is, dear lady.
Your glance from the glazed view-
top of the bus jumps o-
ver this wall. Take your turn
here. Run, skip, with a free
will through wild grass. Rough woo
heath and pagoda, flow
through the palm-houses. Burn

here as you will, you won't
be consumed, so calm is
the light as it moves, slow
as I do, against green
shades and stamens. Leaves wont
to mischief high up, kiss
you with droplets that go
before the attendant's seen.

Peggy Poole

INARTICULATE

my pen is dumb
my hand unmoving
numb, not a single
word will come.
Only your name
echoes in my heart,
my brain,
again and yet again
recurring as the waves'
incessant surging
on the shore –
your name
and nothing more;
in the wind
and in the flame
your name....

Previously published in *Doors*.

MISSING THE DOG

The cat has never known a time
when you weren't there to sleep beside
or use his flap as your look-out
or eat whatever he knocked down
(and share the blame when I raged in).

Last week he searched inside the car
hoping you had moved in there
and that night came a walk with me
to allay his loneliness.
Grief has united us.

Previously published in *Aireings*.

Peggy Poole

CAMP BARBER AT TREBLINKA

My wife stood waiting in the queue
it was a shock to see her there.
Should I tell her what I knew?

Armed guards watched my movements too
I breathed a silent desperate prayer
as she stood waiting in the queue.

As, long ago, I used to do
I now prepared to cut her hair
should I tell her what I knew?

If I survive I will tell true
the cruelties we suffered here.
My wife stood waiting in the queue.

Gas would claim these people who
guessed not their fate, all unaware.
Should I tell them what I knew?

I whispered "Liebchen, I love you"
cropped her curls with tender care
watched her waiting in the queue
could not tell her what I knew.

Previously published in *Lancaster Literature Festival 1991* and *Trusting the Rainbow.*

I.H. Pyves

THE RIGHT TO GENTLE PASSAGE

With fingers wrapped in leaves
I lifted him, golden and gasping,
From cold pavement and onslaught of wind
And placed him in thick green,
That he might think it summer still.

In strong geranium depths
A bruised wing might soothe and
A solitary wasp, last denizen of
Summer, sleep in peace,
So sheltered he dreams it summer still

And passes into such a warmth
Of welcoming sunlit green,
He rises and flexes to flowers
On newly vital wings,
Always to know it summer still.

Eric Ratcliffe

STANDING ON A POINT

Standing on a point, it could be anywhere
my lungs received oxygen, my boots
were Gulliverian, shrunk or blown up,
the sun unreflected from mirrors or jewels
and no angels to create draughts.

Nothing to distract – perhaps at night,
on a canine in the Natural History Museum
– a small dinosaur, the vibrational fright
of school parties long gone, only
a snicker or two from the astral, usually
somewhere west of the ammonites.

It's territorial right, land-stand unable
to be divided, any tears very personal,
running down close under, then lost
in the throat of whatever was once
much more at home in the Lower Cretaceous.

There is much to stand on, needles,
perfectly sharpened pencils, the dorsal
hairs of fox-terriers, I could go on,
but the point is made, I would not pin you
down – but wait for the darkness.

Previously published in *The Man in Green Combs*.

Carole Robertson

HAIKU

Clumps of white snowdrops
Near the poor man's humble house
Raise riches of spring.

Summer's brand new coins:
Shiny yellow buttercups
Fill the field's pockets.

Blackbirds pecking at
Rosy red globes of apples –
First sign of autumn.

Flowering winter
Standing upright in a bowl:
One white hyacinth.

Louise J. Rosenberg

YOU GAVE NO WARNING SIGN

You gave no warning sign that dreadful night
You would in swiftest darkness steal away
Bereft of hope — showing no promised light.

To keep strong friendship's bond you could not fight
A mightier force — which swooped and took you prey;
You gave no warning sign that dreadful night.

In silent hours your sudden secret flight
Strikes with power the part that grief can play;
Bereft of hope — showing no promised light.

Of friendship's autumn days — of calm respite
From stress, from strife: forever lost — astray;
You gave no warning sign that dreadful night.

I wonder: do you feel the sad twilight
Lost friendship spreads; no solace can allay;
Bereft of hope — showing no promised light.

I must forgive you: pity my lonely plight;
I must remember many a happier day.
You gave no warning sign that dreadful night
Bereft of hope — showing no promised light.

Carol Satyamurti

OUR PEACOCK

He was a gloss on that English garden of roses,
banks of blowsy peonies, clipped box.
Ours, because we were his only audience,
and one of us, at least, wanting him to be
an oracle, to fill the sad silence between us
with a fanful of gorgeous air, a sign
richer than the sun's feeble water-dance.

Chivvied by a dozen bloomered bantams,
he dragged his train sulkily in the dust,
a legendary actor in a fit of temperament;
but turned then and, with a shiver of quills,
displayed his gifts to us, no holding back;
Platonic peacock strutting his stuff, all symmetry,
brilliancies, rank upon rank of exquisite eyes.

It wasn't nothing, that we were sharing this
in an English garden smelling of lavender.
But his cold glance told me there's no beauty,
anywhere, to set against old failures of love.
As we left, he lifted himself high into a tree,
and cried out; his voice, broken glass
tearing the heart out of the afternoon.

Previously published in *Striking Distance*.

Barbara Noel Scott

WHITE CYCLAMEN

Cyclamen
inside-out-flower
nun's wimple
virgin queen's crown
how hard it is
to look you in the eye!
Your graceful head resolutely bent down
the stem a leaning curve
your every line
inscribing a posture of effacement.
Why?
Seeing, perhaps, the back swept petals' crown
would leave all bare
the to-be-hidden place,
so your entire being yieldingly bows down
lower and ever lower, to confide
a secrete only earth can share.
Touching the hem of such humility
I have no heart
to lift your face to mine.
I would not dare
to force the secret
of a downcast eye.

Daphne Schiller

THE THREE GRACES (RUBENS)

"The Graces' beauty is of the opulent kind,"
The guidebook reads. Their doughy thighs
Merge into bulging calves, prehensile toes.
Stomachs protrude, buttocks sag,
Breasts collapse like soft ice-cream.
Is this "the subtle play of curvilinear forms"
Or cellulite? Incongruous flowers and drapes
Exude from trees. An inadequate wisp of gauze
Encircles two bottoms. Ripe earth-goddesses,
Their arms entwine. Confident, they pose,
Epitomise "sensual beauty, mellow grace."
Viewing these tranquil naked giants
I picture Rubens, satisfied,
Munching on a dimpled apple.

Previously published in the Ripley Competition anthology.

RODMELL, 1941

I weighted my pockets with stones,
Then walked in slowly. The water was cold,
My clothing sullen. The river flooded
My sterile vagina. The flow of my love
Was always weak. Black spasms of death
Were what I wanted. Its passionate juices
Rushed through orifices. Its bubbles burst
In silvery streams. I was carried away
To the depths of despair. Fear is a language
In which I am fluent.

Previously published in *Success*.

Myra Schneider

ADDRESS

Waking this morning, I fumbled
for the switch, that once-child
bright in my blurred head,
writing her name in joined letters
inside a bumper book
of the Grimms' fairy tales,

and under it two doorknocker fours
by Divert Road. Not interested
in going a long way round
she dived without a pause to Gourock,
Scotland, then The World, THE UNIVERSE,
proud to fix her point in existence.

And possibility was a house of mirrors
where she shook patterns, unlatched
doors to islands, winged populations.
The need for success hadn't shut her in,
nor had she cried for love to stifle
loneliness, found it can hook, wound...

But when I got up this frostbound day
love was somehow my fleece lining.
And I saw the white midwinter moon
thin-skinned as the afternoon,
and myself a dot at the window
of a darkening room circling
a ball of fire in the universe.

Previously published in *The North*.

Jean Sergeant

VILLAGE HIGH STREET

There is a feel of Christmas come too soon.
After a night of frost the mid-day sun
Drenches the street; through open, bright-rinsed doors
Come weather prophets. This small world
Is unaware that I am watching here.

From an advantaged attic perch I see
Soft-scrubbed inhabitants drawn beetling out
In spider leggings, coats of keratin,
Snug babes in buggies, OAPs on bikes,
Loaded with piles of plunder from the shops.

Trucks jog with empty, vulnerable backs
Or jumbled packages, long poles or cans.
Folk winkle into cars' restricted views.
Through traffic tangled in a shepherd's hay
A lady rides upon a dappled grey.

Across from your house a three-floored holly flares,
Lit by the sun to flame in berried bursts,
Which cluster like camelia blooms in spring.
This place, strange yet familiar, is where I've come
To savour all man's essence, balm of home.

Ray Sheppard

BOOKWORM

So many heavy hardback proper books,
A great weight borne by light brown oaken shelves.
Dickens, Shakespeare, Le Carré, volumes in the
    bookcase of cherrywood, red tinted,
        that shines in the morning sun.
Mahogany and walnut also share the burden
    of a hundred years of reading, maybe more.

He calls it his study.
Fingertips delicately trace golden titles
    on the spines;
Fondly handle leather and polished wood, then,
    sadly, switch on the radio for morning story.

She announces that she has to dust
    the sitting rom.

He would like to review his troops,
    The paperbacks on parade on MFI boards
        up in the loft.

But no she says, you won't be safe
    and anyway
I have to take you to the eye clinic today.

Susan Skinner

THE DANCER

You made up your heart early.
Nothing in your pocket but a handful of years.
Put on an ageless suit, a tied bow tie
and patent leather shoes.

Glided in the slippery street,
past tenements where thongs of rain
whipped yellow lamp lights out of shape
and puddles aped the dingy crowd.

From Deptford High to Rottingdean,
you danced and maybe in the stars
you make a ballroom out of death
and still dance in that potent ring

where music influences rain
and poets sing for no reason,
keeping tryst with nightingales
and all the dancing men are king.

Edward Storey

SHADOWS

Here, where the land cranes its thick neck
to stare beyond the water-line, we walk
on stilts to give our spirits height
and stride on legs which lift our weight
above the reedy bog. You'd think
such striving for the light would spunk
our limbs to struggle for the sun
more eagerly than those whose bourn
is half-way there. Not so!
We're frightened, too, of what we do not know.
More effort is required to keep
our bodies raised. We need the cup
of praising if we must look
at things of which we dare not speak.

Living below the level of the sea
gives us the benefit of greater sky
in which to reach for light, but space
can terrify and in our eyes
you'll see the fear of distances.
Yes, we are afraid of boundaries.
Safer to walk this land where clouds
crouch on horizons, where clods
glisten with ancient peat, soaked
by the rain. A man who's looked
upon this land knows his own mind.
If we attempt to rise above the ground
it is to see with sharper eye
the contours of the earth. Maybe
we are afraid, not of the light or sun,
but of those shadows trying to get in.

Previously published in *Fen Boy First*.

Edward Storey

NO DISTANCES, NO GRASS

Within our boundaries was world enough.
Earth had no frontiers we wished to cross.
The fields upheld us and each daily sun
decided always where adventure was.

We watched our fathers working on the land,
the farmers' trailers wilting under corn;
then mothers in coarse aprons and large hats
riddling potatoes near an open barn.

We saw the seasons marry and unfold
through habit, ritual, or commonsense.
There was no need to question or explain
the narrow streets or meadows' bright expanse.

But when the gates were opened and the town
let half its children out to go abroad,
we lost our freedom and the skies closed in
like walls we could not climb or then break down.

The world was suddenly too small and old,
there were not distances, no grass, no air.
The furrows, rivers, games and days of light
were in a country we had known elsewhere.

As exiles then we told ourselves that we
were driven out like tenants with bad debts,
when what we know is that we chose to go
and being wrong is what we can't accept.

Previously published in *Fen Boy First.*

Sean Street

TUTOR MELANCHOLY
(Naga-uta after a Degree Ceremony)

Today reprieved me
from making you memories
if only for a moment: a last seminar.
And I, surrogate parent
just now have drunk and
pretended hope with you; bright
possibilities
asked to be believed as life,
smiling all the while,
looked on poignantly at us,
and the clock stepped back
tactfully, its time coming.

After wine, silence.
Now you've moved on from today,
I become a ghost
fading as your days here sink,
turned (perhaps) to memory.

Sean Street

HENRY VAUGHAN, 1695-1995
Silex Scintillans

Beyond the monitor's blank perfect blue
splinters the uncertain spring

I notice two birches have not found the will to leaf
      (this is over technology's head)

          You should never place computer screens against the light

these two things —
this is why
(I think I now see)

I make white hieroglyphs on this blank perfect blue
             black on this perfect white

out of such order no perfection thank God —

        there is no manual for this

            but this —

      It is breaking makes flint flash

Nan Strength

I HAVE A RING

I have a ring
a ring that lies around
that lies around my neck
this ring so bright
so brightly worn
my ring my neck
it binds my love
I flow into this ring
so bright it glows
so tight it grows
O ring my ring
my brightly shadowed ring
my ring of life of love
of fine and polished gold
my love so polished
fine and bare
O ring of love
I have a ring

Frances Stubbs

MUNRO BAGGING

I should explain, to those who do not know;
Munros are Scottish mountains of great height,
And every day, I'm climbing a Munro.

When you have climbed three thousand feet or so
Above the world, the air is clear and bright.
I should explain, to those who do not know,

How rare and beautiful the flowers grow,
And you can watch the soaring eagle's flight.
And every day, I'm climbing a Munro

In sun and wind, or sometimes rain and snow,
Or swirling mist, when all the world is white.
I should explain, to those who do not know,

How clouds roll back, and suddenly, below
Are tiny farms; a river's thread of light,
And every day, I'm climbing a Munro.

But every dusk, I seek the camp fire's glow,
Content that, resting in its warmth at night,
I should explain, to those who do not know,
That every day, I'm climbing a Munro.

Margaret Tims

BUTTERFLIES IN THE STOMACH

The cat sat by the buddleia, and watched.

The buddleia stretches, spreading its rich plumes
Like proffered wine.

The air stirs, and a whirr of wings
Descends and dances in atomic sequences
Circling and dipping, sipping the lip of pleasure.

Eye of Peacock, flash of Admiral, milk-powdered
Cloud of Cabbage White,
Pale satellite moons, caught in the sunburst
Of the burning bush.

Jehovah claps his paws.
A torn wing floats, soft-landing on a leaf,
Antennae trail in dislocated pain,
A furry body crumples, broken-backed.

The universe dissolves in panic air.
And on the ground a little pile of pale moon-dust
Gathers in stricken silence.

The cat sat by the buddleia, and waited.

David Van-Cauter

SOAP OPERA

The plates were so bright, he could see his face in them.
The suds washed off, they stood, half-cocked and wet.
"Coffee would be nice," he heard above the TV,
Dried his hands on a paper towel, watched her cigarette.

The smoke dilated as it blew between them,
Thick as milk. "No sugar. Black."
It was too hot. He slipped and spilt it everywhere.
"Well, wipe it off," she said. The plates dripped on the rack.

Her tears were flowers. The petals lit her face.
"I'm sorry, love. I won't do it again."
He wiped — her eyes drifted away.
The pupils danced with images. The coffee left a stain.

Doreen Van-Cauter

DEPARTURE

Shimmering sea sinking into moonlit shadows
Ghostly green furrows dredge the surface
Like eerie etchings scaring stone
In long neglected country churchyards.

A boat caught – frozen – trapped
Cannot break from homely moorings
To challenge an unknown open sea.
Slender lengths of moonsilk rope
Assume a tinsely twilight strength
A twitchy tenuous link to land and home.

Breathless – we wait
A single sign – an unseen hand
Expels, releases – lets us go
The landmass drifts away.

Ted Walter

CARSHALTON PARK
for All Saints School 15.11.95

This a leaf that's falling lightly,
Lightly falling to the ground.
If we listen very quietly
Will we hear it make a sound?

This a tree that's standing proudly,
Proudly standing – losing leaves.
Are the sounds it whispers loudly
Proof a tree in Autumn grieves?

This a wind that's blowing strongly,
Strongly blowing in the park.
Do we think, however wrongly,
Scattered crows are fiercely dark?

This the rain and this the sunlight,
Sunlight spun through fleeting rain.
Is the curve of double rainbow
Symbol of the gifts we gain?

This a star that shines so brightly,
Brightly shining way up high.
Were we to watch it like this nightly
Would we learn the reason why?

Envoi:

Leaf and tree and wind and rainbow;
Children still and listening,
Searching for their own true wisdom,
Crow and starlight beckoning.

This the day and this the pleasure;
Eyes that brighten, eyes that cry;
Here the place where angels measure
All the joys of poetry.

Mildred Wickrema

SPACE

The earth spins round
In space,
Empty, dark,
Cold, freezing.
Then man shoots in,
Protected by steel.
Alone?
Not for long.
Another steel shuttle
Comes close; opens,
A Russian nods out
So does the American.
They shake hands.
Space no longer empty.
The earth
Spins round unheeding.

Jane Wight

THE GUNS

Beautiful and doomed
This lone cock pheasant
Very slow paces
A daybreak fragment
Of western Herefordshire:
He drums at the corner
Of his empty field,
Glinting in red and green,
Staring down the landscape's fall,
Being bold and small and doomed
Like cavalry before the guns.

Remember, in the coming dusk,
Before the North Sea flows back,
Doomed and very beautiful
A guillemot – a young one –
Resting on the pebbles
With a brown smear of oil
Like a tag pinned on the heart
To guide the marksmen, but
The mark alone kills and slowly,
And the bird is quiet and still,
Touching on enforced sleep.

Its narrow head and the whole
Back are dark, just turned with
The white of Indian silver.
Simply to look is coldness,
Yet handling vain impertinence,
So slowly with a pinion
From some lost, safer bird
Stroke down the head and back,
Outline the narrow head.
For a moment the beak opens.

The defenders are falling;
We do not even see the guns
We hold.

Peter Williamson

THE SMALL BAKER
Rue St Honoré

The small baker carried bread;
he was as humble as rain.
The work of some seems a piety
not given to us all to share
in quite the same way.
But in this way or that
there is an excellence for all to find,
each in his own fashion,
not measured by the Slave of Michelangelo
or Chartres, built firm and clear
over the Druids' well,
but grown from anyone
in a small way daily.

You can find it
in the smell of coffee, freshly made,
or of the baker's oven,
where in the evening's dull warmth
the cricket cries
improvident;
we feel his small cry
is ours.
His ceaseless song
with our small light
defeats the darkness
of the grave.

Previously published in the *New York Times* and *New York Times Book of Verse*; also broadcast on Radio 3 (*Poetry Now*) and in French on BBC Français.

Frances Wilson

TOUCHING UP THE BLOODSTAINS

Years after he'd moved out,
moved in with his girl-friend
she still couldn't face up
to repainting his bedroom.

When they'd first stripped it,
awaiting the baby, they'd unpeeled
the whole history of the house
in layers of paper, right back

to victorian roses. It felt
like walking on graves, disturbing
more than the imprint of hands
pressed into the brickwork.

Finally she had to accept it.
Eight years of adolescent male
graffiti whitewashed. It took over
a week, and not only the reading.

But she refused to do up
the bathroom, the burn on the sill,
worn faint as a thumb-print,
where he'd rested a cigarette

while mending the cistern,
that first weekend they'd left him
alone, and he'd painted his bedroom
ceiling black, with bloodstains.

Previously published in *The London Magazine*.

Andrew Young

LAND OF NO RETURN

He is naked inside his head, with no remembered land
to return to, having been back before but only
to gawp and pilfer.

He knows he is approaching death, but does not know
if there is anything there of his.

On the hillside, the wind blew against him
and he felt the days approach when his legs
would no longer respond or carry him:
neither to Eden nor the Land of Nod.

His letters of credit bear the arms
of nations which have fallen apart;
his money is in a currency nobody wants.

He can never return, and lives in the border town
he calls his head, where no-one leaves
and no-one arrives.

NOTES ON CONTRIBUTORS

Mary Adcock has been writing articles and short stories since the 1950s and more recently has turned to poetry. She is a Quaker and has contributed to *The Friend*.

Elizabeth Argo is the pen name of Beth Smith. Started writing in her fifties and has contributed poems to several national publications. Winner of Ver Poets Open Competition 1988 and joint winner Freda Downie Memorial Competition 1995. Now retired, she is writing a book on education.

Pat Arrowsmith was on the staff of Amnesty International for 24 years and has herself been a prisoner of conscience; CND vice-president. She has won poetry prizes and published four illustrated verse collections; has also published three novels and a book of fiction-cum-memoirs *I should have been a Hornby train* (1995).

Kenneth Bailey has had verse broadcast and published in Britain and America; his collections include *Time and the Island, Distant Music* and *The Sky Giants*. He favours fantasy and science fiction; lives on Alderney in the Channel Islands.

Marjorie Baker is a retired teacher of English. Compiled, contributed and partly illustrated the Kent and Suffolk volumes of *Poet's England*; enjoys pottery and painting as well as poetry.

Patricia Ball was for many years art therapist at a St Albans mental hospital where she also instituted regular poetry sessions for the patients, out of which two books of their poems were published. In retirement she has self-published her own poems, requesting only small donations to charity in return for copies; these are available from Ver Poets, of which Pat is a life-member.

Margaret Banthorpe has a degree in Zoology and is a contributor to *Wildlife Matters* and other journals. Poems have been published in various magazines as well as one collection *Ring upon Ring* (Nat. Poetry Foundation 1992).

Roy Batt is a retired lecturer in anatomy at the Royal Veterinary College. Has won several prizes with Ver Poets and composes haiku whilst walking the dog on Hampstead Heath; his collection *Taking Liberties* was published in 1995.

Mary Blake lives in a tiny cottage high up in the Chilterns, communing with 'the green man' and baking her own bread. Joined Ver Poets in 1992; her poems have been commended in competitions, displayed on the London buses and published in magazines.

Rachel Blake has taught in London, Spain and Africa and now lives in Surrey. She was included in *New Women Poets* (Bloodaxe 1990) and her collection *Lifedrawings* came out in 1994; has also published short stories.

Grace Blindell trained as a nurse and later taught mathematics. Following two years' voluntary service in the Gaza Strip her poetry collection *Have you wept, Samson?* was published by Quaker Peace and Service in 1986.

Rosemary Bosworth is a retired medical secretary living in Sutton Coldfield. Her poems have appeared in two anthologies, *The Mexican Hat Dream* (1993) and *West Midlands – Poetry Now* (1994).

Geoffrey Bould edited a compilation of writings by prisoners of conscience, *Conscience Be My Guide* (Zed Books 1991) and since joining Ver Poets in 1993 has had poems published in various journals. A member of the Society of Friends, he lives in Watford.

John Bourne lived in Grenada for two years where he was inspired to write by the work of Derek Walcott. His poems have appeared in several anthologies and a few have been translated into Russian.

Suzanne Burrows lives in Letchworth and is a former co-editor of *Spokes* poetry magazine. Her poems have been published in magazines and she has twice been a prize-winner in the Bridport poetry competition.

Maggie Cain was born in Cheshire and lives in South Yorkshire, where she is a hospital social worker. Started writing eighteen months ago, after thinking about it from childhood.

Marjorie Carter began seriously writing poetry six years ago, when she joined Ver Poets. Second prize Crabbe Memorial Poetry Competition 1991; first prize 1992. Joint third prize Ver Poets Open Competition 1994. Her poems have appeared on the London buses and in various magazines. Lives in Ipswich.

Margaret Caunt has published three books of poetry and is on the editorial panel of *Envoi*. She has a degree in zoology and is married to a research chemist. Lives in Welwyn Garden City; other interests are singing, painting and psychic research.

A.C. Clarke has published poems in a number of magazines and anthologies; has won Ver Poets Open and poemcard competitions. A member of the 'Poetry for Joy' group and 'still trying to find a truthful voice'.

Gladys Mary Coles runs Headland Publications and is a tutor in Imaginative Writing at Liverpool University and John Moores University. She has won first prize in a number of national poetry competitions as well as other awards for literature. Publications include *Leafburners* (Duckworth 1986), *The Glass Island* (Duckworth 1992) and *The Poet's View: poems for paintings* (1996). Also a literary biographer and has published two studies of Mary Webb.

John Cotton's collections *Old Movies* and *Kilroy was Here* (Chatto & Windus) were respectively a recommendation and choice of the Poetry Book Society. His last full collection is *Here's Looking at You Kid* (Headland); poetry for young people includes *Two by Two* (with Fred Sedgwick) and *Oscar the Dog and Friends* (Longmans). He is President of Ver Poets and chairman of Toddington Poetry Society.

John Coutts has published several collections including *Words beyond Words*, *A Garland for the Passion* and *A Sackful of Plays and Poems for Christmas*. His poetry show A Box of Surprises is performed in schools, clubs, theatres and churches. He has won awards at folk festivals and has translated Pushkin's poetry from Russian.

Penelope Cutler now lives in north Yorkshire and was formerly co-ordinator of Letchworth Writers Group, where she was prize-winner in a local competition. Her poems have appeared in a number of local publications and in *Poetry in Motion — London*.

Alan Dunnett read English at Oxford before going to drama school, and has been a theatre director for a number of years. Formerly based in Nottingham, he is now Acting Tutor at the Central School of Speech and Drama in London. His poetry has appeared in magazines and anthologies and a collection *Hurt Under Your Arm* was published by Envoi in 1991.

Judith Everitt, now in her fifties, writes for friends and ' my own entertainment'. Some poems have been published in magazines, including the winner of the *Outposts* fortieth anniversary competition, as well as a booklet *Fandango* (Pickpockets, Hastings).

Gillian Fisher attended secondary school in Billericay and now lives in Lincolnshire. Since 1970 has published poems in various magazines and anthologies; won a runners-up prize in *Peace & Freedom* competition in Spalding in 1996.

Dorothy Francis has a B.Ed. degree and 'has always written poems' without seeking publication; was included in *Behind the Spade* (Poetry Now, 1994). Also interested in choral singing; belongs to several art societies and a WEA literary group.

Joan Fry has been ordained in the Church of England and is assistant priest in Bridport, Dorset. Has contributed to several magazines and anthologies including *New Christian Poetry* and *New Poetry 4*.

Muriel Gibson's poetry developed out of an early interest in verse speaking. Her poems have been published in various little magazines and anthologies, and in a collection *First Impression* (Envoi Poets); joint first prize in Ver poemcard competition.

Ray Givans has won prizes in several Ver Poets competitions; winner of Jack Clemo Memorial competition 1995. Has read at literary festivals in Belfast and featured on local radio. A member of Poetry Ireland and the Fellowship of Christian Writers.

Daphne Gloag read classics and philosophy at Oxford and has since worked as a medical journalist. Poems have been published in various journals and anthologies and broadcast on Radio 3. First collection *Diversities of Silence* published 1995 (Brentham Press). Married to Peter Williamson (*qv*).

Hilda Groom spent her teenage years in Canada and later trained as a nurse in England. Has written scripts for the Saskatchewan Historical Society; poems have been published in this country and America. Now lives in London.

Elsie Hamilton has been writing poems since childhood and has been published in a number of magazines and anthologies, including Ver Poets publications and *North West Anthology* (1994). Lives in Manchester.

Alan Hardy is director/teacher at an English language school for foreign students. Poems published in a number of magazines; 2nd prize Hastings National Poetry Competition 1994; first collection *Wasted Leaves* 1996.

Joyce Haynes has been a member of Ver Poets since 1975. Poems have been published in several anthologies and some have won prizes in Ver competitions. She remains, by temperament, a 'closet poet'.

Christopher Highton has been writing for about five years and has been successful in three open poetry competitions; work published in various poetry magazines and in *The Countryman*. Lives at Beckenham.

May Ivimy had her first poem published in school magazine; since graduated to *Time & Tide, Tribune, Poetry Review* and Radio 3 and 4; collections published by Headland, Mandeville and Brentham presses. Wearing other hat (May Badman's), fully occupied with Ver Poets; also full-time wife, mother, grandmother... *Motto*: 'Let your pen heal, not poison'.

M.A.B. Jones graduated from Bristol university and later qualified as a barrister, working mainly in educational administration. Contributor to many poetry magazines and anthologies, including *Voices of Today* (John Murray, 1980); six collections published. Awarded prizes at South Wales Eisteddfod 1986, 1992 and 1994; and Minsterley Eisteddfod 1991 and 1995.

Pauline Keith has worked in Africa, the Middle and Far East, Holland and Canada. Now a creative writing tutor living in Lancaster. Many poems published; joint 3rd prize Ver Poets open competition 1990.

Hannah Kelly was born in Poona, India and read English at Birkbeck College, London university. Four volumes of poems published, latest *The Promised Land* (Autolycus Press 1994). Currently chairman Camden Poetry Group and has edited five Camden anthologies; citation of Meritorious Achievement for Services to Literature 1994.

Robert Knee lives in Norfolk and teaches religious education. Prize for best poem on a rural theme, Norwich Writers Circle open poetry competition 1996; also published in *Haynonymous Anthologies*, Hay on Wye.

Gillian Knibbs graduated in English and philosophy at Leicester; now teaches English in Hertfordshire. Has been published in *Spokes* magazine and won prizes in various competitions including Ver Poets autumn competition 1994.

Lotte Kramer was born in Mainz, Germany and came to England as a child refugee in 1939. Did a variety of jobs whilst studying art and art history at evening classes and has held one-man shows. Since starting to write poetry in 1970 has been widely published in England, USA, Canada, Eire and Germany; poems also broadcast on radio and TV. Six collections published, latest *The Desecration of Trees* (Hippopotamus Press) and *Earthquake and Other Poems* (Rockingham Press). Lives in Peterborough.

Keith Lewis lives in Anguilla in the West Indies. Poems published in magazines and anthologies. Highly commended for BBC Wildlife Poet of the Year award 1992; third joint prize Orbis Readers award 1995; commended Ver Poets competition 1995.

Mari Louth-Cook read history at London university; MA research degree in education, Southampton university. Has taught all age groups and lectured in sociology in higher education. Memoirs *Up hill and down* accepted for National Life Story awards, British Library collection 1994. Married and widowed twice, lives in Harpenden. Hobby: buying land and building houses.

Susanne Lutz lives in Switzerland and teaches English. Has contributed short stories to Swiss magazines and two English stories have won prizes in a Swiss competition. Poems published in Canada and USA.

Kevin Maynard is a teacher now working in the St Albans area after many years in London.

W.A. Mellors is a Lancastrian by birth but has lived for more years in St Albans. Started writing poetry in later life and poems have apeared in several anthologies.

David Message has worked in the printing industry and started writing poetry in 1987. Nine small collections published, latest *The Blue Mountains* (1996). Has travelled widely and lives at Sandy, Beds.

John Mole has published several poetry collections, most recently *Selected Poems* (Sinclair Stevenson 1995), and a volume of review essays *Passing Judgements* (Bristol 1989); a new collection for children *Hot Air* (Hodder) appears this summer. Recipient of Gregory, Signal and Cholmondeley awards. Vice-president of Ver Poets and head of English at St Albans School.

Julian Mounter has been writing poetry seriously since 1985; poems published in several magazines and anthologies, most recently *Triumph House Poets of 1996* and *Words of Worship*. Lives at Somerton in Somerset.

Olive R. Nathan was born and brought up in Edinburgh; worked as a teacher and later an academic librarian in London. Poems published in magazines and with Stratford Poets. Now lives at Woodford Green, Essex.

Ruth Partington was educated at London university and the Sorbonne, and by travel. Has taught French and done free-lance photography. Poems and articles published in various magazines; Carlsberg prize 1973. Special interest in gypsy lore; translation of Sandra Jayat's *Nomad Moons* published 1995 (Brentham Press).

Brian Louis Pearce, librarian and lecturer, has published a number of poetry collections, including *Gwen John Talking* (2nd ed. Stride 1996) and *Thames Listener* (Univ. Salzburg Press 1993); also fiction and studies of Victorian and Edwardian poets, based on lectures at the National Portrait Gallery.

Peggy Poole's sixth collection was *Trusting the Rainbow* (Brentham Press 1994); has since edited *Poet's England: Cumbria* (Headland 1995) and an anthology of railway poems *Marigolds Grow Wild on Platforms* (Cassell 1996). Lives on Merseyside and this year retired as Poetry Consultant for BBC North.

I.H. Pyves has been published in a number of anthologies including *South East Voices* (Anchor Books 1994) and *The Haunting Muse* (Siren Books 1994); also in Ver Poets publications. Formerly chief librarian at a college of higher education, now living in Kent; special interest in animal welfare.

Eric Ratcliffe edited *Ore* magazine 1955-95 and has published a number of booklets. Most recent poetry *Fire in the Bush* and *Anthropos* (both Univ. Salzburg Press); *Odette* and *Sholen* (both Astrapost). Now working on *Paranormal Pointers* (psychic research).

Carole Robertson wrote her first poem at age eight and saw her first one printed two years later in school magazine. Since published in a variety of magazines and anthologies, including Sotheby's International Poetry Competition anthology (Arvon 1982). Lives in Swindon.

Louise J. Rosenberg is a retired teacher; obtained BA Hons from Open University. Poems have appeared in *Jewish Quarterly* and other journals; in Ver Poets anthologies and 'on the buses'; awarded prize in St Albans Arts Festival.

Carole Satyamurti, poet and sociologist, teaches at the University of East London and the Tavistock Clinic. Poems published in a wide variety of magazines and anthologies and broadcast on radio and TV. First prize National Poetry Competition 1986; Arts Council writers' award 1988; many times workshop tutor for Arvon Foundation and elsewhere. Three poetry collections published, latest *Striking Distance* (1994), a Poetry Book Society recommendation.

Daphne Schiller has an MA in creative writing from the University of East Anglia and teaches for the WEA. Poems published in magazines and anthologies and broadcast on radio and TV. Prize-winner in several competitions; also writes short stories and articles.

Myra Schneider has been widely published in journals including *The Observer, The Independent, Critical Quarterly* and *London Magazine*; also in anthologies, most recently *The Dybbuck of Delight, poems by Jewish women* (Five Leaves 1995). Two novels for teenagers and one for children published by Heinemann. Lives in north London and teaches severely disabled adults in a day centre.

Barbara Noel Scott was born in Cambridge on Christmas Day 1913 and has been publishing poetry since the early '60s. Contributor to many magazines and anthologies, including *Poetry from East Anglia* (ed. G. Scurfield 1978). Awards include 2nd prize Envoi Open Poetry Competition 1995. Four booklets published, latest *Seasons and Celebrations* (Envoi Poets 1993).

Jean Sergeant has been published in *Outposts* and *Weyfarers* magazines and in anthologies. Prizes in three Ver Poets competitions and first prize Ver poem-card competition 1995. Started 'Poetry for Joy' group in memory of her husband Howard Sergeant, meeting each summer in Ludlow. Lives in Surrey.

Raymond Sheppard recently retired from the Hertfordshire ambulance service. Short stories and poems published in house magazines; prizes in two Irish competitions. Produced his own collection *White Bridge Poems* in 1995.

Susan Skinner is poet, calligrapher, children's writer and creative writing tutor. Winner of Kent & Sussex Open Poetry Competition and (twice) Julia Cairns Competition. Published a number of children's stories and two poetry collections. New book for young people *The Dream Cave* now in production.

Edward Storey has published several prose works on life in the Fen-country, including his autobiography *Fen Boy First*. Fifth poetry collection *Last Train to Ely* published 1995. Winner of Ver Poets Open Competition 1993 and Wells Literature Festival 1993. Regular contributor to poetry magazines and frequent broadcaster.

Sean Street has published five poetry collections, latest *This True Making* (KQBX Press). Other publications include *The Wreck of the Deutschland* (Souvenir), *The Dymock Poets* (Seren) and *A Remembered Land* (Michael Joseph). His play Honest John won the Central TV Drama Award in 1993. Regular broadcaster on radio 2, 3 and 4; Associate Senior Lecturer in Media Studies at Bournemouth University.

Nan Strength was born in Nigeria and bred in Northern Ireland. Now living in England, writes ' in the gaps between living'.

Frances Stubbs contributed to the Poetry Society's *Voice of Youth* magazine in the 1960s and twice won the May Cattell competition. Poems later appeared in *Makaris*, magazine of Durham university poetry society. Now writing again after a gap of thirty years; three poems accepted in anthologies.

Margaret Tims has had varied writing, editing and publishing experience. Founder and director of Brentham Press, which publishes the *Poet's England* series of regional verse (now in association with Headland Publications) as well as individual authors in both poetry and prose.

David Van-Cauter recently completed an MA in modern literature at the University of Kent, where he was short-listed for the T.S. Eliot prize for poetry; also edited an anthology and broadcast a radio show dedicated to student writing. Has contributed to anthologies and magazines and now works as a free-lance editor.

Doreen Van-Cauter has a BA degree in English and MA in modern social history. An academic tutor, recently completed a grammar book for children. Contestant on 'Mastermind' in 1996; specialist subject 'the Chartist movement'.

Ted Walter is a free-lance tutor with adult classes in creative writing and 'reminiscence work'; also visits schools throughout south-east England as 'Poet in school'. New collection of poems in preparation for 1996 publication.

Mildred Wickrema was born in Sri Lanka; BA degree from London university and MA from Clark university, Massachusetts. A teacher in several countries including Singapore and Ghana before her last post at Townsend School, St Albans. Wrote and illustrated her reminiscences in *Brown Teacher, Big World*; also produced two booklets of verse.

Jane Wight, East Anglian Celt, lecturer and author of books on pre-1550 brick and decorated tiles. Also much poetry in self-published and -artworked booklets. Lives in Norwich.

Peter Williamson has been a social worker and careers adviser. Poems widely published in this country and United States and broadcast on Radio 3 and BBC World Service. Three collections published, latest *Footholds* (Brentham Press 1996). Married to Daphne Gloag (*qv*).

Frances Wilson is a writer, painter and workshop tutor. Awards include 2nd prize National Poetry Competition 1990, 1st prize Rhyme International competition 1991 and 1st prize Nottingham poetry competition 1995. Two collections published, latest *Close to Home* (Rockingham Press 1993).

Andrew Young writes 'compulsively' with 'spasmodic forays into print'. Recently self-published his *Lost Art of Astronomy*; has translated much work of Georg Trakl.